To my dad, my personal cheerleader, who believes
I will conquer the world, one snack break at a time. —R.G.

Lucky Rabbit Publishing LLC
1421 Calhoun Street
Columbia, South Carolina 29201
www.luckyrabbitpublishing.com

Book design by Gabriel De La Torre

978-1-966829-12-6

Printed in China

LUCKY RABBIT

LITERACY

Hands-On abcs

By Rachel Gitzen

Lucky Rabbit Writing Series

Hands-On abcs: Building Strong Hands for Easy Letters

Dear caregivers and educators,
Here are the answers to some questions you may have about this book.

In what order are the letters presented?

First, letters with straight lines, l, i, t, are presented, then, letters with curved lines, o, a, d, b, p, q, c, e, u, f, h, g, j, n, m, r, s, and finally, letters with diagonal lines, k, x, v, w, y, z.

Why are the letters presented in this order?

The written alphabet is shown in a different order than the traditional A-Z sequence to enhance learning effectiveness. This method emphasizes mastering letters with straight lines first, then simple curves, and then diagonal lines. This aligns with motor skill development and builds confidence in writing.

Why lowercase letters?

Although uppercase letters are generally easier to write, we see and use 95% lowercase letters versus uppercase. Learning lowercase letters and their corresponding sounds first provides a strong foundation for developing reading and writing skills.

What are all these lines and pictures?

When teaching children how to write, it's important to make the process fun, visual, and consistent. In order to achieve this, each line has been given a name and an image to help the child visualize in their mind, before writing it.

Consistency Children hear the same terms every time they write; helping them build memory and confidence.

Visualization Instead of copying a letter, children imagine how it is built from shapes they already know.

Engagement Naming the lines makes writing less intimidating and more playful.

What are fine motor skills?

Also called dexterity, our fine motor skills are the coordination we have in the small muscles in our hands and feet. Fine motor skills give us the ability to use our hands, fingers, feet and toes to manipulate objects.

Why are fine motor skills important?

Our fine motor skills allow us to write, type, draw, turn door handles, use silverware, button our clothes, zip zippers and many other daily activities.

What are the Off-the-Page activities?

Off-the-Page activities are designed to make learning engaging and fun! These hands-on experiences help children develop letter recognition, phonemic awareness, and fine motor skills using everyday items found at home or easily accessible materials. By bringing learning to life beyond the pages of a book, these activities create an interactive and enjoyable way for children to explore letters and sounds while building essential skills.

For tips and tricks, follow us on Instagram @luckyrabbitliteracy

About the author.

Rachel Gitzen is a passionate educator with a Bachelor of Arts in Early Childhood Education from the College of Charleston. With more than 15 years of combined experience as a nanny and teacher, she has devoted her career to nurturing children's creativity, curiosity, and love of learning through everyday play.

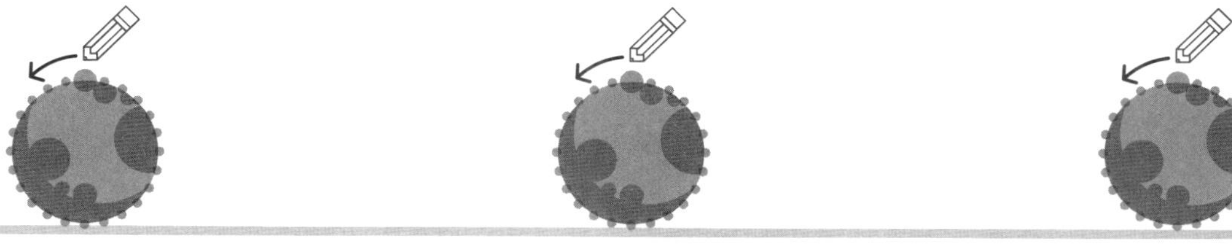
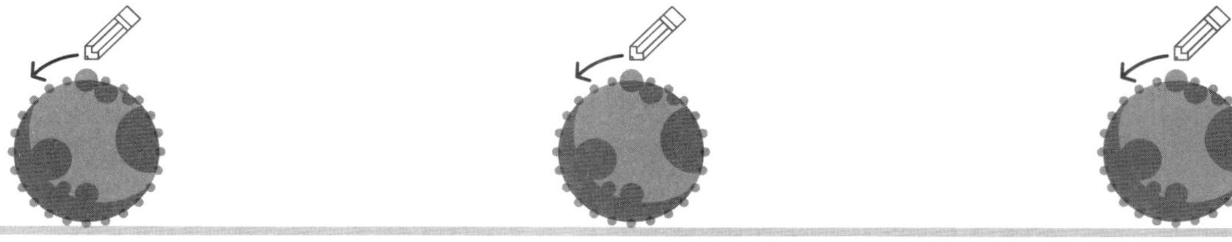
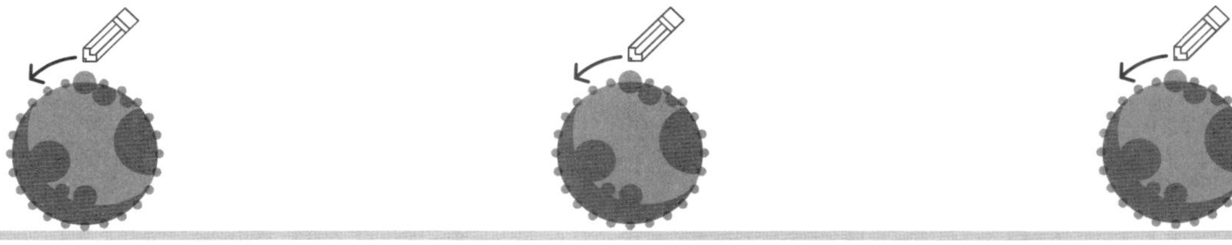
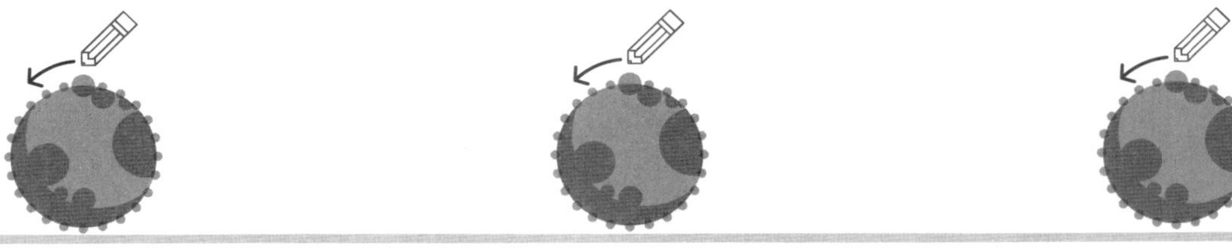

lock

Off-the-Page Activity

Tearing Paper

Have the child tear colored paper into strips. Save torn paper for another day.

Off-the-Page Activity

Letter Hunt

Give the child an old magazine or newspaper. Call out a letter and have the child find and point to that letter. Extension: Point to a letter and have the child say the name and sound of the letter.

iguana

Off-the-Page Activity

Blocks

Give the child blocks and have them imagine something, then build it. Extension: Build an object using up to five blocks, and have the child copy it.

Off-the-Page Activity

Water Writing

Give the child a paintbrush and cup of water. Let them practice their lines and letters on the concrete.

Need to stay inside? Add a tablespoon of salt to a cup of water and paint on dark paper.

toucan

Off-the-Page Activity

Color Sort

Have the child sort torn colored paper strips by color into cups.

Off-the-Page Activity

Bath Letters

Provide the child with foam letters. Have the child stick the letters, one by one, to the shower wall, while saying the letter name and sound.

o

otter

Off-the-Page Activity

Disappearing Art

Add a few squirts of paint to a gallon-sized storage bag. Seal the bag and tape it to a flat surface. Have the child smoosh the paint around the bag, then draw in the paint using their finger.

Off-the-Page Activity

Letter Match

Write lowercase letters on 1-inch pieces of masking tape, and stick them around the house.

Write uppercase letters on a sheet of paper. Have the child stick the lowercase letters on top of their corresponding uppercase letters.

a

ant

Off-the-Page Activity

Puzzle

Have the child put together an age-appropriate puzzle. Accompany and encourage, but don't interfere.

Off-the-Page Activity

Torn Paper Letter Art

Using a pencil, draw a large letter on a sheet of construction or printer paper. Have the child glue torn pieces of paper along the lines of the letter. Glue tip: Just a dot, not a lot!

d

dog

Off-the-Page Activity

Stickers

Have the child peel and stick stickers onto a sheet of paper.

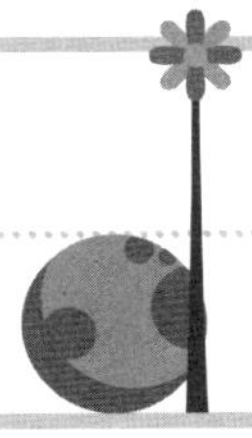

Off-the-Page Activity

Spray Bottle Letters

Write letters on concrete using chalk. Call out a letter or letter sound and have the child spray that letter with a water bottle.

b

bat

Off-the-Page Activity

Pipe Cleaners and a Colander

Have the child practice sticking pipe cleaners in the holes of a colander. You can also use dry spaghetti.

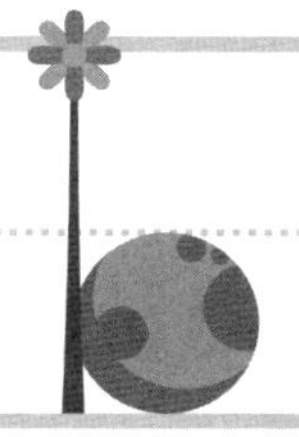

Off-the-Page Activity

Alphabet Pasta Hunt

Pour dry alphabet pasta into a bowl or onto a flat surface. Call out a letter/sound for the child to find or have them pick the letter and tell you the letter and sound.

p

pen

Off-the-Page Activity

Play Dough

Give some play dough to the child and play with it together. Make a car, dog, flowers, etc.

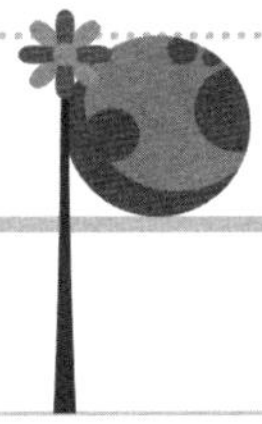

Off-the-Page Activity

Hide and Seek

Fold dry alphabet pasta into play dough and have the child find the letters.

q

queen

Off-the-Page Activity

Beads in a Bottle

Have the child place beads into the opening of an empty water bottle. Extension: Have the child count or say colors as they do this.

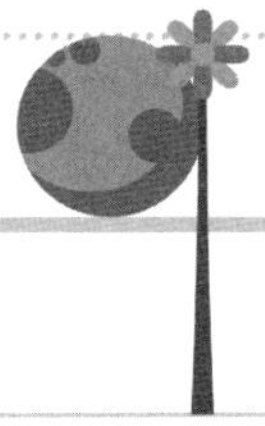

Off-the-Page Activity

Letter Ball

Write letters on scraps of paper, and tape them to the wall. Call out a letter/sound and have the child throw a soft ball at the corresponding letter.

c

cat

c

c

c

Off-the-Page Activity

Spray Bottle Play

Let the child explore and practice using a spray bottle outside or in the bathroom.

c

①

①

Off-the-Page Activity

Tray Writing

Pour a thin layer of salt onto a sheet pan. Have the child draw and write in the salt, using their finger.

Carefully swish the pan from side to side to clear the writing.

e

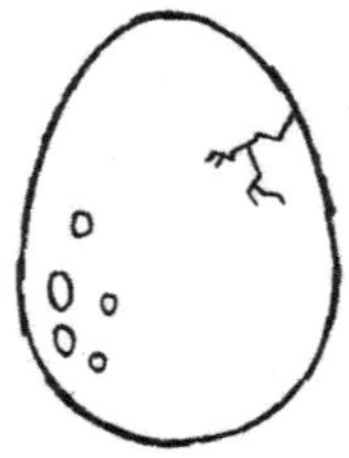

egg

Off-the-Page Activity

Crumple Paper

Give the child small pieces of paper (2"/5cm) and have them crumple the paper into little balls.

e

①→ ↑②

①→ ↑②

Off-the-Page Activity

Letter Hunt on the Town

While running errands or walking around, point to a letter and have the child name the letter and say its sound. Focus on one letter at a time.

up

Off-the-Page Activity

Chalk Lines

Give the child chalk and have them draw or write on the concrete. Have them practice vertical, horizontal, and diagonal lines.

Off-the-Page Activity

Fly Swatter Smash

Write letters on scraps of paper and place them on a flat surface. Using a clean fly swatter, have the child swat the letter/sound you call out.

fish

Off-the-Page Activity

Play Dough Cut

Have the child smash or roll some play dough flat. Using a toothpick, draw a line in the play dough. Have the child use child-safe scissors to cut the play dough along the line.

Off-the-Page Activity

Flour Trace

Pour a thin layer of flour on a flat surface and allow the child to draw or write with their finger.

Practice lines and letters.

h

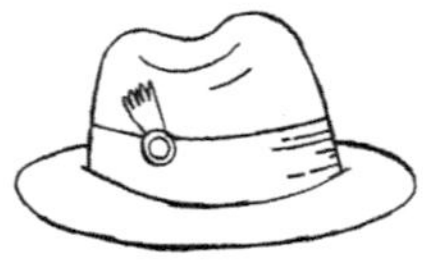

hat

Off-the-Page Activity

Water Cups

Give the child a tub of water and let them experiment with pouring water in and out of multiple plastic cups over the tub.

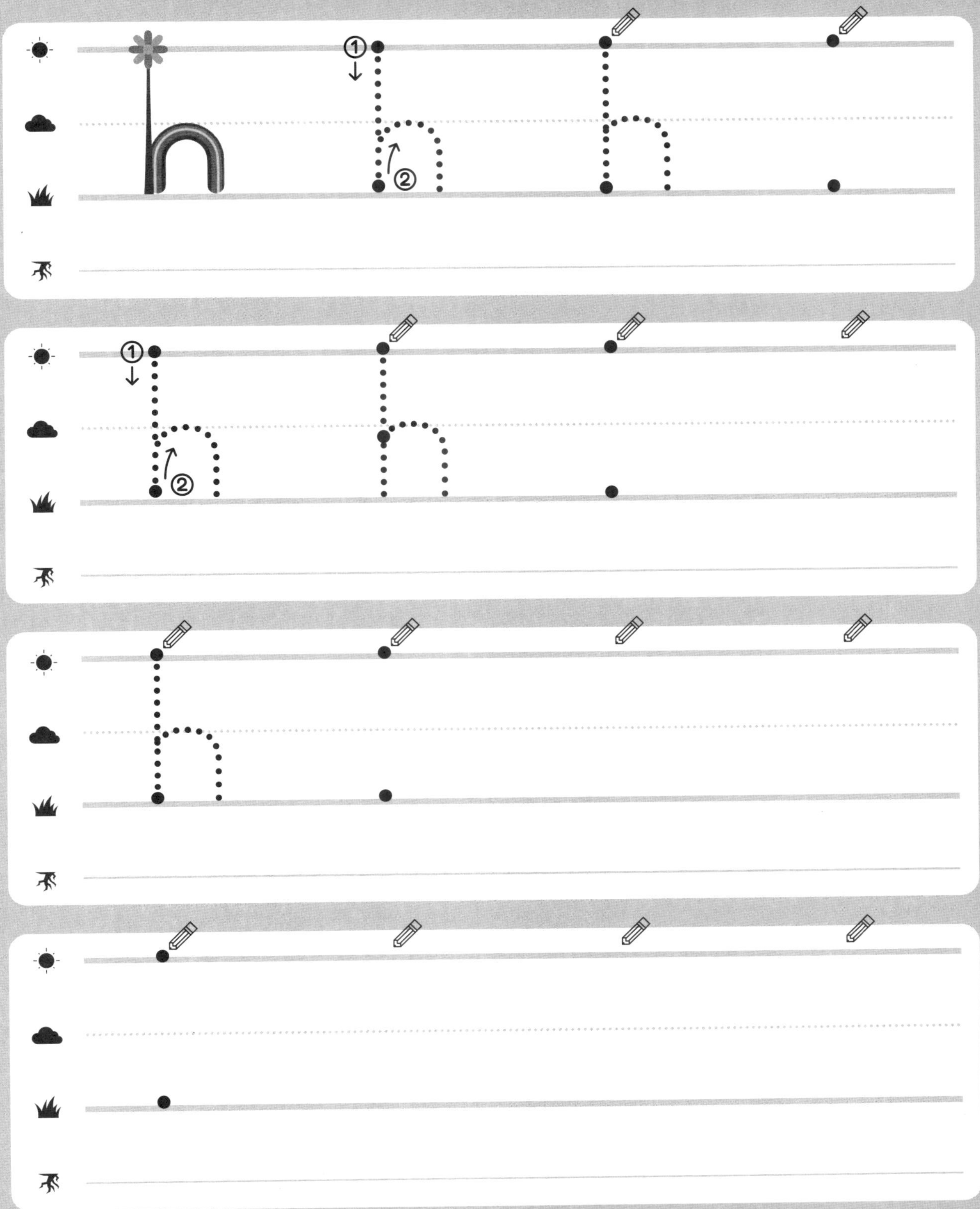

Off-the-Page Activity

Bubble Wrap Pop

Find some bubble wrap with large bubbles, and write a letter on each bubble. Call out a letter or sound and have the child pop the bubble with the corresponding letter using their fingers.

g

goat

Off-the-Page Activity

Beading

Have the child thread beads onto yarn or a shoelace. Extension: Have the child make a pattern, starting with ABAB (Ex: red, blue, red, blue).

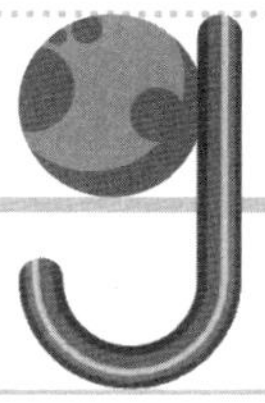

Off-the-Page Activity

Alphabet Memory

Cut printer paper into eight pieces. Choose four letters the child knows and write each one on two pieces of paper. Place the letters face down. Have the child pick up two pieces at a time to try to match the letters. Add more pairs of letters as they learn them.

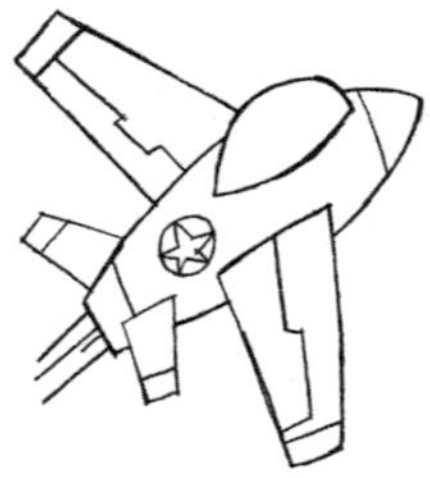

jet

Off-the-Page Activity

Buttons

Gather a button-down shirt and show the child how to button a button. Button the button together. Then have the child practice buttoning. If the buttonhole is too tight, try a different shirt!

Off-the-Page Activity

Cotton Swab Art

Write a letter on a piece of construction or printer paper. Tape the piece of paper to a flat surface. Put small amounts of paint on a plate. Have the child dip a cotton swab into the paint, then make dot pictures and letters on the paper.

net

Off-the-Page Activity

Hole Punches

Guide the child on how to hold and use a one-hole punch. Allow them to create as many hole punches as they'd like. Extension: Use different colors of paper. After creating lots of hole punches, have the child sort the colors.

Off-the-Page Activity

Magnetic Alphabet

Using magnetic letters, have the child find the letter you call out by name or sound. Or point to a letter and have the child tell you the name and sound. Extension: Make CVC (consonant, vowel, consonant) words like cat, bat, mat, etc.

m

mop

Off-the-Page Activity

Thread it

Have the child stick pipe cleaners in the holes of a colander, then thread round cereal onto the pipe cleaners. Make it colorful. You can also use dry spaghetti noodles.

Off-the-Page Activity

Rock Hunt

Go on a rock hunt. Pick up small rocks (big enough to write on); write letters on each rock and practice the names and sounds of the letters.

r

rat

Off-the-Page Activity

Torn Paper Art

Have the child use torn paper and glue to create a picture. If needed, assist the child by drawing a simple picture on the paper (flower, train, sun, etc).

Off-the-Page Activity

Alphabet Jump

Write big letters on the sidewalk with chalk. Call out a letter or sound and have the child jump onto that letter. Extension: Have the child copy the letter on the sidewalk with chalk.

s

sun

Off-the-Page Activity

Shaving Cream Lines

Spray a small amount of shaving cream onto a washable surface. Have the child spread the shaving cream into a thin layer and practice drawing vertical, horizontal, and diagonal lines, along with circles.

Off-the-Page Activity

Copycat

Write a letter or draw a shape with a highlighter, and have the child trace the letter/shape with a pencil.

k

key

Off-the-Page Activity

Scissors

Allow the child to practice cutting, using paper and child-safe scissors.

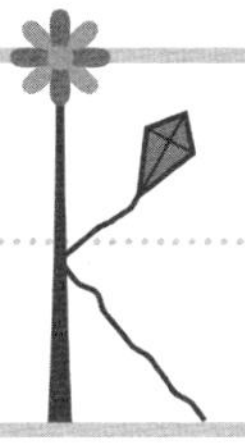

Off-the-Page Activity

Play Dough Letters

Have the child create letters out of play dough and practice saying the name and sound of each letter.

x

fox

Off-the-Page Activity

Bead Sort

Place a handful of beads in various colors into a bowl. Have the child sort the beads by color into smaller bowls.

Off-the-Page Activity

Letter Blocks

Write letters on blocks and have the child build using the letters you call out. OR write uppercase letters on one block and lower case on another and have the student match upper and lowercase letters.

v

vase

Off-the-Page Activity

Finger Painting

Tape a piece of paper to a flat surface. Using washable finger paints, allow child to paint whatever they want.

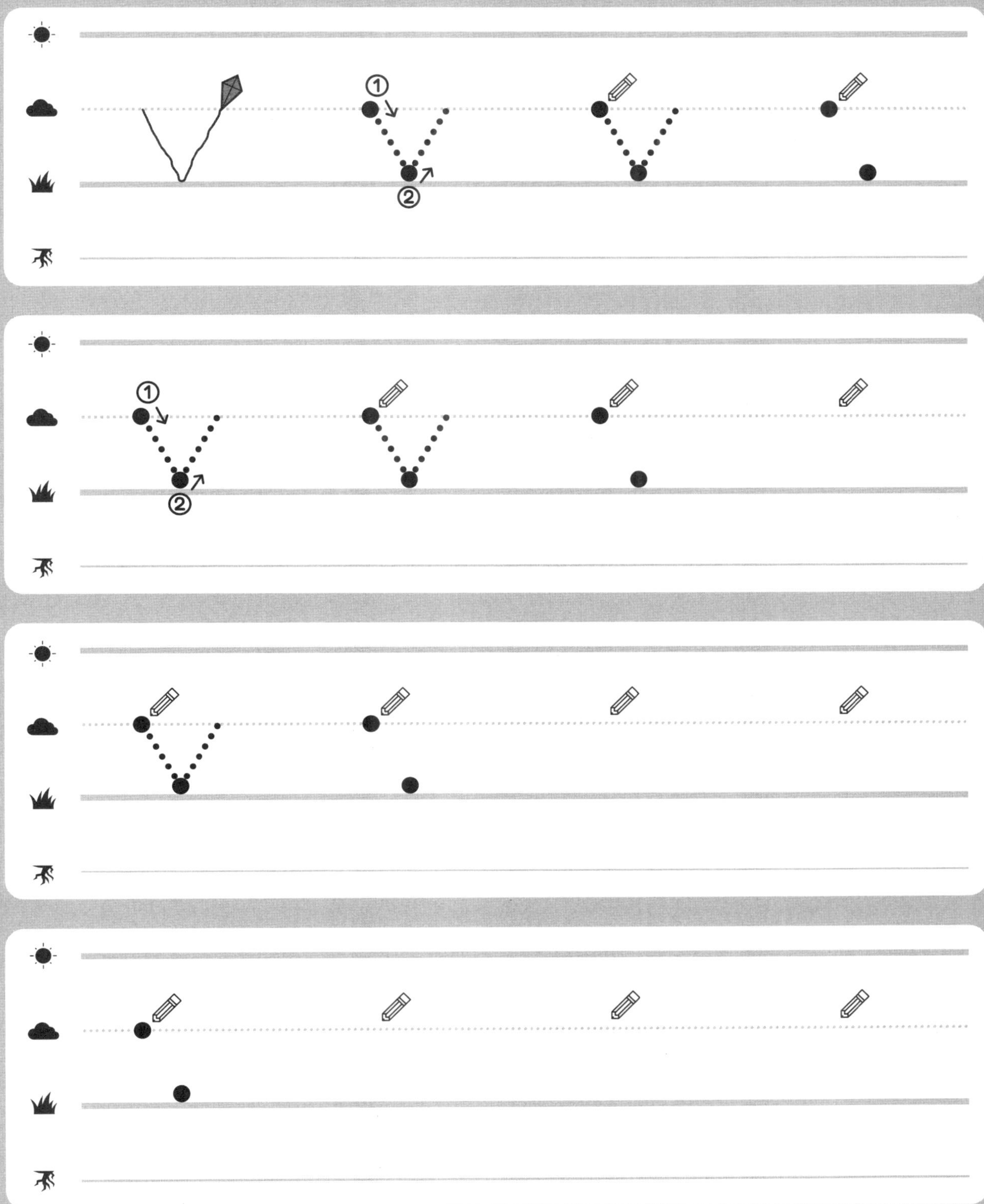

Off-the-Page Activity

Seek the Letters

Fill an empty water bottle half full with dry alphabet pasta and colorful plastic beads. Have the child twist and shake the water bottle to find letters. Have them say the letter and sound they find.

w

worm

Off-the-Page Activity

Skewer Threading

Have the child secure a wooden skewer with a ball of play dough on a flat surface. Have the child thread round cereal onto the skewer. Tip: Instead of a wooden skewer, you can use dry spaghetti.

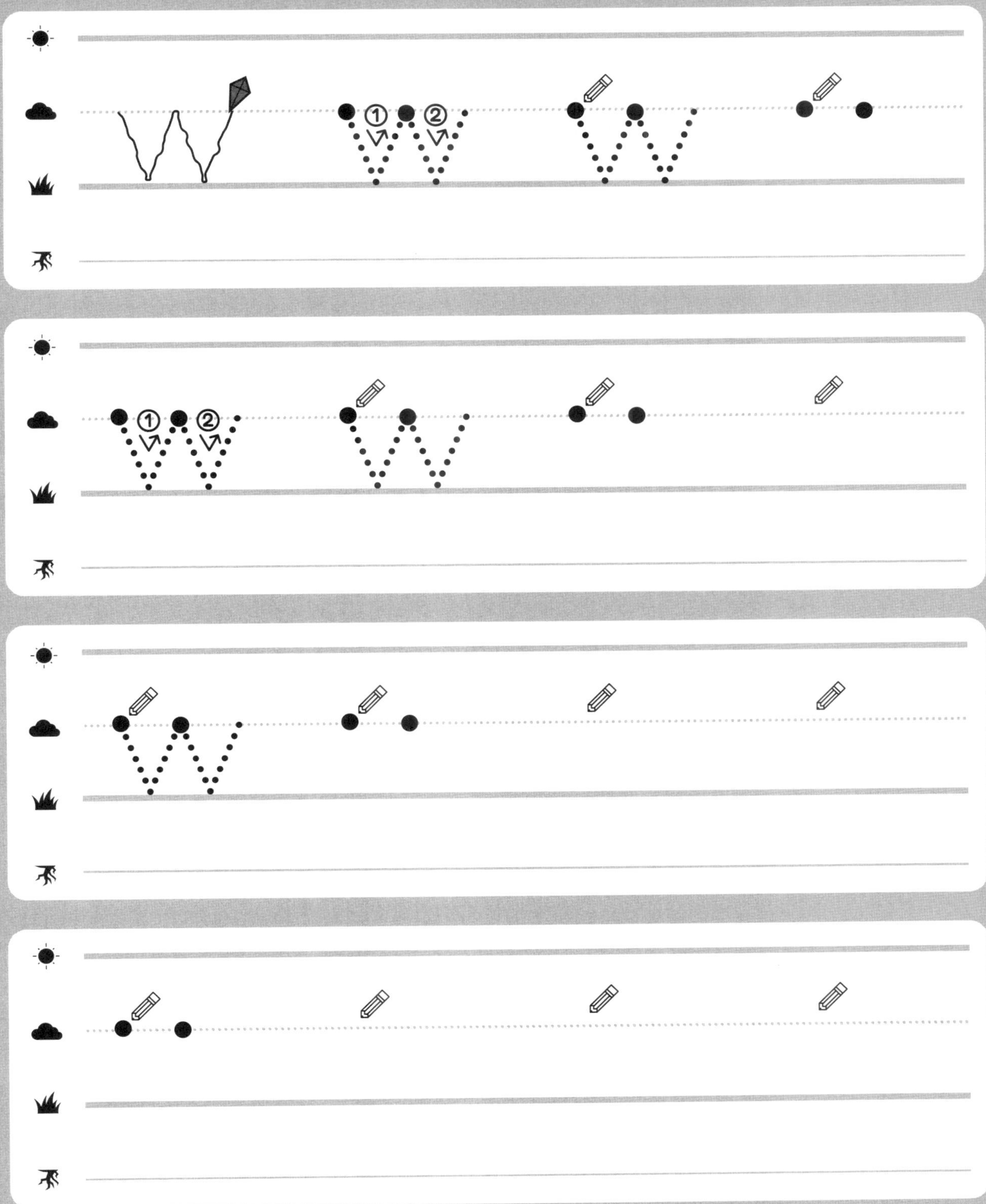

Off-the-Page Activity

Play Dough Letter Smash

Have the child roll play dough into small balls. Using a letter stamp, have the child stamp a different letter on each ball. Once all of the balls have a letter, call out a letter/sound and have the child smash the corresponding ball of play dough.

y

yo-yo

① ②

① ①

② ②

① ② ① ②

Off-the-Page Activity

Color Dropper

Using eight clear cups, water, food coloring, and an eye dropper, have the child explore how to make colors. Fill four cups with an inch of water. Add two drops of food coloring to each cup (one color per cup). Have the child use the eye dropper to add different colors together in the empty cups. Guide them to make colors.

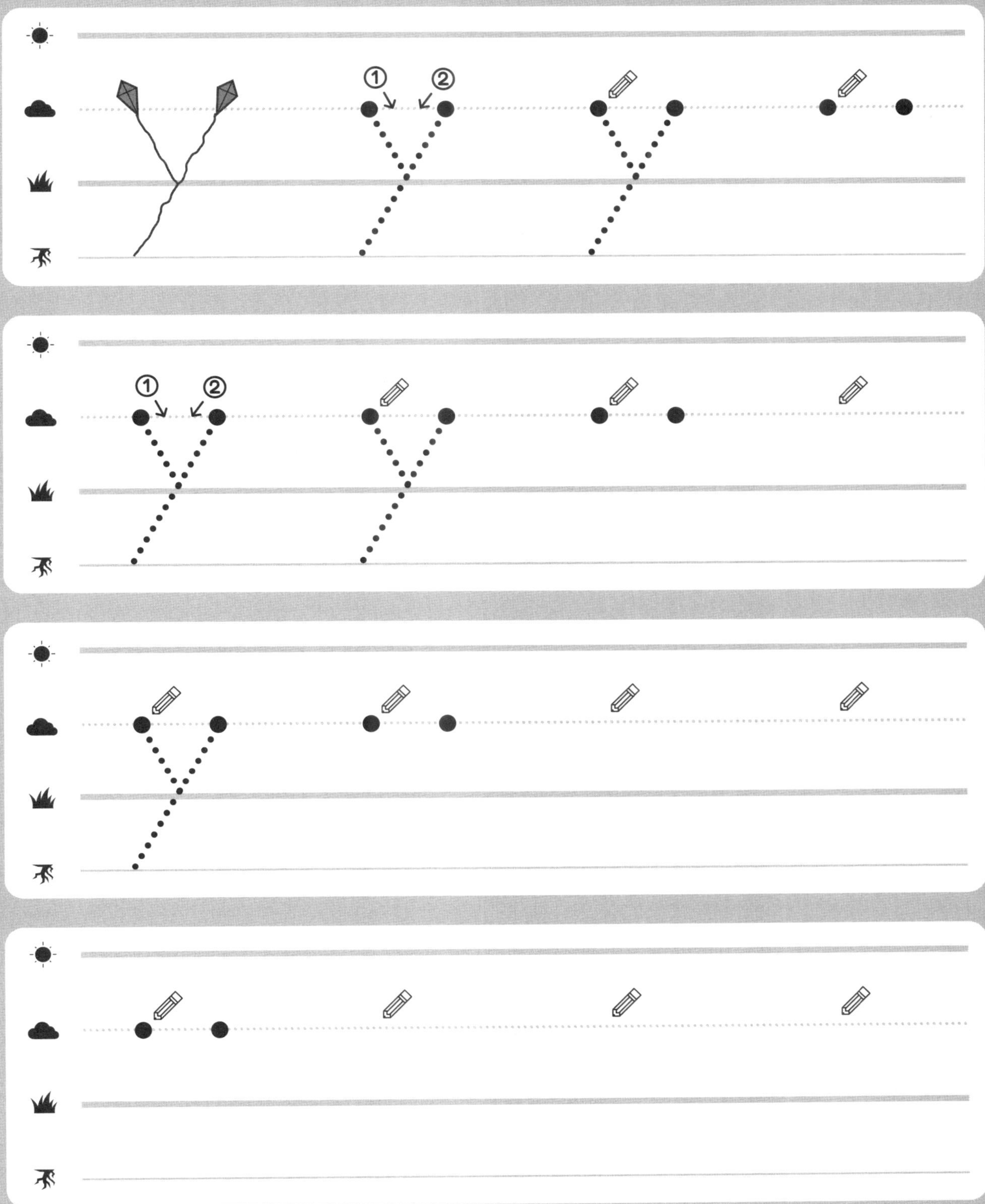

Off-the-Page Activity

Finger Paint Letter

Tape a piece of paper to a flat surface. Have the child practice writing their lines and letters in finger paint or with a paint brush.

z

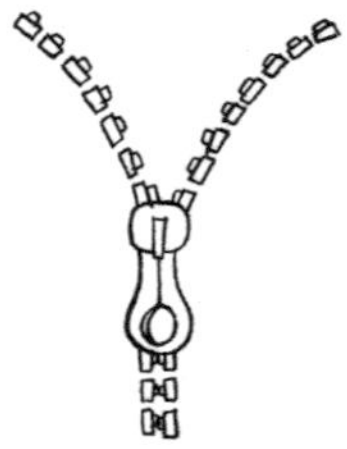

zipper

① → ② ③ →

① → ① →

② ②

③ → ③ →

Off-the-Page Activity

Muffin Tin Sort

Have the child use a clothespin or small tongs to pick up pom poms and sort them by color in a cupcake tin.

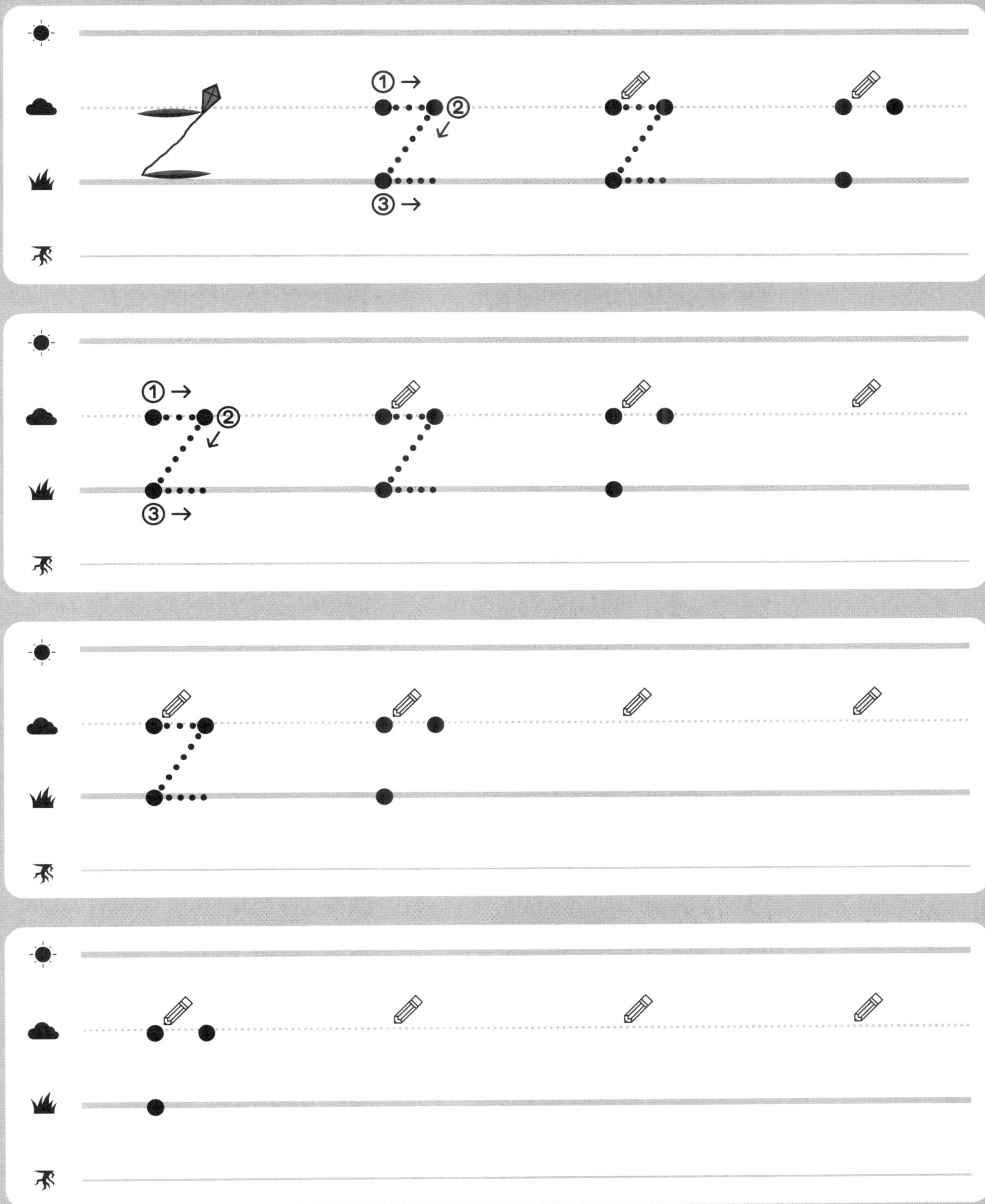

Off-the-Page Activity

Garage Letters

Draw lines the length of a toy car on a spare piece of paper or cardboard. In each "parking space" write an uppercase letter; on each toy car write a lowercase letter. Have the child match the car to the parking space.